Bible reflections
for older people

15 The Chambers, Vineyard
Abingdon OX14 3FE
brf.org.uk

Bible Reading Fellowship is a charity (233280)
and company limited by guarantee (301324),
registered in England and Wales

ISBN 978 1 80039 135 2

Acknowledgements

Scripture quotations marked with the following abbreviations are taken from the version shown. Where no abbreviation is given, the quotation is taken from the same version as the headline reference. NIV: The Holy Bible, New International Version (Anglicised edition) copyright © 1979, 1984, 2011 by Biblica. Used by permission of Hodder & Stoughton Publishers, a Hachette UK company. All rights reserved. 'NIV' is a registered trademark of Biblica. UK trademark number 1448790. GNT: The Good News Bible published by The Bible Societies/HarperCollins Publishers Ltd, UK © American Bible Society 1966, 1971, 1976, 1992, used with permission. NKJV: The New King James Version®. Copyright © 1982 by Thomas Nelson. Used by permission. All rights reserved. ESV: The Holy Bible, English Standard Version, published by HarperCollins Publishers, © 2001 Crossway Bibles, a division of Good News Publishers. Used by permission. All rights reserved. NLT: The Holy Bible, New Living Translation, copyright © 1996, 2004, 2007, 2013. Used by permission of Tyndale House Publishers, Inc., Carol Stream, Illinois 60188. All rights reserved. TLB: The Living Bible copyright © 1971 by Tyndale House Foundation. Used by permission of Tyndale House Publishers Inc., Carol Stream, Illinois 60188. All rights reserved.

Page 34: 'Third Sunday after Easter' © Victoria Field. Used with kind permission. Pages 35–36: Extract from *How to be a SuperAger* © Angela Lucas. Used with kind permission.

Every effort has been made to trace and contact copyright owners for material used in this resource. We apologise for any inadvertent omissions or errors, and would ask those concerned to contact us so that full acknowledgement can be made in the future.

A catalogue record for this book is available from the British Library

Printed and bound in the UK by Zenith Media NP4 0DQ

Contents

About the writers

Margot Hodson is director of theology and education for The John Ray Initiative (JRI), an educational charity bringing together scientific and Christian understandings of the environment in a way that can be widely communicated and lead to effective action. She is also a vicar in Oxfordshire and on the board of Grove Ethics Editorial Group. **Martin Hodson** is a plant scientist, an environmental biologist and operations director for JRI.

Clare O'Driscoll was a runner-up in *The Upper Room* writing competition of 2020. After 13 years in Bible translation administration, she has been giving Spanish and French tuition, writing occasional articles for Christian publications and providing press support for a local youth charity. She is also on the team of volunteer editors at *magnet* magazine. She lives in West Sussex with her family and loves the sea.

Derek Morgan is a recently retired IT professional, after spending over 30 years in software development roles. Having been a Christian for 40+ years, he knows his gifting will never be as a preacher or evangelist, but his God-given passion is facilitating those who are. He lives on the south coast of England.

Emlyn Williams worked for Scripture Union for many years, in various places and roles, particularly relating to schools. He is a writer of many individual and group Bible materials. Following three years working with an Anglican church in Southampton, he retired and now lives in Norfolk, where he continues to write.

From the Editor

Welcome to this new collection of Bible reflections.

The saying *solvitur ambulando* – 'it is solved by walking' – is attributed to various sages, most commonly St Augustine of Hippo. The one-time Bishop of Durham, H.C.G. Moule (1841–1920) added two words to the saying: *solvitur ambulando cum Deo*: It is solved by walking with God.*

In late October 2020 I walked part of the South West Coast Path. This was to be a walking retreat – time to reflect, time to go deeper. As it turned out, wind, hail, mud, missing signposts, slippery rocks and rain that turned my maps to pulp meant that my only thoughts were how to stay upright and how to find my way. Meditation, no. Reflection, no.

Two contributors to this issue, SuperAger Angela Lucas and poet Victoria Field, have walked the Camino, the ancient pilgrim route to Santiago de Compostela. For both of them – and for me – the real wisdom of our walks came only after we'd arrived at our destination and loosened our boots.

At the end of her book about her Camino pilgrimage,** Victoria writes: 'Something changed. My faith deepened. The veil is increasingly thinner and I see through it more often.' Whether we knew it at the time or not, it is solved by walking with God.

Go well

---

* *Outlines of Christian Doctrine*, chapter 3, 'The Doctrine of the Father'.
** *Baggage: A book of leavings* (Francis Boutle Publishers, 2016).

Using these reflections

Perhaps you have always had a special daily time for reading the Bible and praying. But now, as you grow older, you are finding it more difficult to keep to a regular pattern or find it hard to concentrate. Or maybe you've never done this before. Whatever your situation, these Bible reflections aim to help you take a few moments to read God's word and pray, whenever you have time or feel that would be helpful.

When to read them

You may find it helpful to use these Bible reflections in the morning or last thing at night, but they work at any time of the day you choose. There are 40 reflections here, grouped around four themes. Each one includes some verses from the Bible, a reflection to help you in your own thinking about God, and a prayer suggestion. The reflections aren't dated, so it doesn't matter if you don't want to read every day. The Bible verses are printed, but if you'd like to read from your own Bible that's fine too.

How to read them

- **Take time** to quieten yourself, becoming aware of God's presence, asking him to speak to you through the Bible and the reflection.

- **Read** the Bible verses and the reflection:
  - What do you especially like or find helpful in these verses?
  - What might God be saying to you through this reading?
  - Is there something to pray about or thank God for?

- **Pray**. Each reflection includes a prayer suggestion. You might like to pray for yourself or take the opportunity to think about and pray for others.

A wing and a prayer

Martin and Margot Hodson

Birds appear at the very beginning of the Bible, on the fifth day of creation when God said, 'Let the water teem with living creatures, and let birds fly above the earth across the vault of the sky' (Genesis 1:20, NIV). As we go through the Bible, we see them in flight and nesting, both behaving more honourably than God's people and acting badly. The last mention of birds is in a rather bloodthirsty passage from Revelation 19:21 (NIV): 'The rest were killed with the sword coming out of the mouth of the rider on the horse, and all the birds gorged themselves on their flesh.'

Bird are sometimes used to paint the background to a passage, and sometimes used to illustrate theological truths. Leviticus 11:13–19 lists 19 bird species considered unclean and not to be eaten. Bats would make 20, but we now know they are mammals, not birds. This list illustrates a problem of writing about birds in the Bible: different translations often give quite different species. To simplify, our reflections follow the species named in the NIV.

So come with us as we explore what our feathered friends can tell us about God, humanity and the wider creation.

Isaiah 40:31 (NIV)

The eagle

But those who hope in the Lord will renew their strength. They will soar on wings like eagles; they will run and not grow weary, they will walk and not be faint.

Breakfast with the eagles was a magical experience in the Alpujarra Mountains. Our holiday apartment had a small terrace overlooking the valley, and most mornings we would watch a pair of Booted Eagles as they circled upwards on thermals, their majestic wings spread wide. It seemed effortless and yet we knew they had terrific strength.

Losing strength is a terrible thing. It may be physical because of illness or increasing age, or it may be emotional because life's knocks have just become a bit too much. Whatever our situation, we can turn to the Lord for strength. We may look longingly at the effortless flight of the eagles, but God will strengthen us in ways we cannot know. God's strength comes through the Holy Spirit. He is with us at all times and understands our weaknesses. He knows our deepest desires, and his healing touch gives us all that we need to make us whole.

Experiencing God's power in our lives is an inner strengthening that enables us to face the future. We might not be running in the Olympics, but we will be running the race for Christ.

■ **PRAYER**
Dear Lord, only you can give us strength when we are weak. Help us to trust in you for the strength that we need each day. Amen

Zephaniah 2:14 (NIV)

The owl

Flocks and herds will lie down there, creatures of every kind. The desert owl and the screech owl will roost on her columns. Their hooting will echo through the windows, rubble will fill the doorways, the beams of cedar will be exposed.

Our reading forms part of a short prophecy by Zephaniah concerning what will happen to the city of Nineveh in Assyria because of their arrogance and pride. This is one of the passages where we are uncertain exactly which species the birds are, but whatever the writer intended, in the Bible these species are always associated with desolation and lack of human habitation. One can imagine the haunting cries of these birds across the levelled city. The picture is one of total destruction after a devastating attack by an opposing army.

Whenever I (Martin) think of desolate landscapes, it takes me back to a visit I made many years ago to Sudbury in Northern Ontario, Canada. This was the site of historic nickel and copper mining, which had so polluted the land that hardly anything could live there. Just a few dead tree stumps rose out of the blackened landscape, and there was an apocryphal story that the Sudbury wastelands had been used to practise moon landings.

War and environmental degradation can both lead to desolate landscapes. We think of wars damaging people, but they can be catastrophic for the natural environment too.

■ **PRAYER**

Lord, we pray for both peace and better care for your creation. Amen

1 Kings 17:6 (NIV)

The raven

The ravens brought him [Elijah] bread and meat in the morning and bread and meat in the evening, and he drank from the brook.

Wild camping has become popular in recent years. Pitching a tent right out in the wilds and being able to make your home surrounded by nature, even for a short time, somehow enables a reconnection with the earth God made and from which we were formed.

Foraging in the wild is also fun, though very challenging if that is going to be your only source of food. Elijah had just stood up to the wicked King Ahab and warned him that there would be drought in the land. Knowing he was now in danger, the Lord led him to a safe ravine where there was water but little food. Here, the ravens fed him. One wonders what culinary delights the ravens came up with.

Sometimes we need to stand up for things that are difficult and we fear the consequences. But we can trust in God. If he could supply Elijah with a safe haven and all his needs from his creation, he can also provide you with a haven and support if you need to take a stand. If there is something that is not right, don't be afraid to share it with someone you trust. And be at peace – God cares.

■ **PRAYER**

Lord Jesus, give us courage to stand up for what is right and trust that you will support us and bring us through difficulties. Amen

Jeremiah 8:7 (NIV)

The stork

Even the stork in the sky knows her appointed seasons, and the dove, the swift and the thrush observe the time of their migration. But my people do not know the requirements of the Lord.

Jeremiah wrote his prophecies to warn Judah that if the people did not change their evil ways, disaster would await them and their capital, Jerusalem, would be destroyed. In our reading, Jeremiah compares the wisdom of birds with the foolish ways of the people of Judah.

White storks pass through Israel in the spring and the autumn on their long migrations from Europe to southern Africa and back. Only a small number breed within Israel. So Jeremiah would have been used to huge flocks of storks flying over twice a year. The stork and the other birds mentioned know when to migrate, but the people did not know what God wanted.

So the stork, dove, swift and thrush all have perfect timing, and they know when to leave their summer quarters and when to return. How can we emulate these birds in their timing? How can we know the right time to take up or give up a commitment or responsibility, to move house or to retire? God will help us with all these decisions and more. If you have a big decision to make at the moment and are uncertain about the timing, pray that God will show you.

■ **PRAYER**

Lord, please help us with our timing and guide us in your ways. Amen

Job 39:13 (NIV)

The ostrich

The wings of the ostrich flap joyfully, though they cannot compare with the wings and feathers of the stork.

Job 39:13–18 is a short description of ostrich behaviour, which forms a part of the famous passage in which Job is shown how little he understands about the natural world. The passage is not very complimentary about the way ostriches lay eggs on the ground and do not look after their young very well, but then returns to the feathers in verse 18, where we can see their advantage: 'Yet when she spreads her feathers to run, she laughs at horse and rider.'

As we have already seen, storks can use their wings to migrate, often thousands of miles. In contrast, the ostrich is flightless and its wings can seem weak and puny. But then, the ostrich has a peak running speed of 60 mph, and it uses its wings for balance, particularly when changing direction. They are also used in courtship displays. So maybe they are not so useless after all.

Is an Olympic gold medallist better than a Nobel Prize-winning scientist? Is a church pastor more valuable than a nurse? Is a politician of greater worth than a cleaner? We make these sorts of comparisons all of the time and they can often be very unfair. In God's eyes everyone is useful and everyone is special.

■ **PRAYER**
Lord, help me to avoid making unfair comparisons. Amen

Luke 12:6 (NIV)

The sparrow

Are not five sparrows sold for two pennies? Yet not one of them is forgotten by God.

House sparrows seem such common birds, yet, in the UK, there has been a decline of over 70% in their numbers during the last 40 years. A range of factors has led to this sharp drop in population, including a decrease in invertebrates, who are sources of food, and the loss of habitat.

When creatures are common, it is easy to take them for granted, and it is a shock when we find them disappearing so rapidly. Our consumer lifestyles and the actions of governments and big corporations has led to a massive decline in wildlife across our world. We have forgotten them, yet not one of them is forgotten by God.

As we grieve the loss of wildlife, we need to ask God for his forgiveness and for ways in which we can help to reverse this decline. A simple action, such as putting up a nest box, can make a huge difference to one family of sparrows. If you have a garden, allowing a corner to go wild can help replenish food sources for birds. Overall, we know that God cares for sparrows as well as caring for us. We need to care too.

■ **PRAYER**

Dear Lord, it grieves us when we see your beautiful creation damaged by our actions. Help us to find ways to repair your world and help us to value sparrows and all that you have made. Amen

Mark 14:72 (NIV)

The rooster

Immediately the cock crowed the second time. Then Peter remembered the word Jesus had spoken to him: 'Before the cock crows twice you will disown me three times.' And he broke down and wept.

The cock crowing was our daily wake-up call. The unused hen coup in our huge vicarage garden was providing a holiday home for a cockerel while his young owner was away with her family. We enjoyed his distinctive 'cock-a-doodle-do's through the day and it all added to the country atmosphere.

For Peter, the sound was a very different wake-up call. He had bravely followed Christ after his arrest, but hid his identity out of fear. As the sound pierced through the grey light of dawn, Peter suddenly realised he had let Jesus down. He simply broke down and wept.

A wake-up call is a shock. We suddenly see things from a different perspective and realise we have made a huge mistake. It may be that we have let someone down, and the consequences of our actions, or inactions, are starkly revealed when it seems too late to go back. Like Peter, we may feel like weeping, longing to bring back what has been lost.

After Jesus rose from the dead, he met with Peter and forgave him. Like Peter, we are offered a pathway to forgiveness through the cross that leads to restoration and eternal life.

■ **PRAYER**

Dear Lord, thank you for your gift of forgiveness. As you forgave Peter, please forgive me. Amen

Jeremiah 17:11 (NIV)

The partridge

Like a partridge that hatches eggs it did not lay are those who gain riches by unjust means. When their lives are half gone, their riches will desert them, and in the end they will prove to be fools.

The bird translated 'partridge' in our present verse is *Kore* in Hebrew, a caller, named because of its distinctive harsh call, with the most likely species in Israel being the sand partridge or maybe the chukar. The GNT paraphrases the first part of our verse as, 'The person who gets money dishonestly is like a bird that hatches eggs it didn't lay.' Nobody seems too sure where this idea of a dishonest bird first arose, but the naturalist, Bartholomew, writing in 1535, said the partridge 'is so guileful that the one stealeth the eggs of the other'. As far as we can determine, this is not a common behaviour, but the birds are occasionally 'dishonest'.

However, it is immediately obvious that this dishonest behaviour does not pay off in the end. The birds hatching from the stolen eggs are said to recognise the call of their natural mother and to follow them instead: 'their riches will desert them'. And so it is with us. Dishonest behaviour never pays off. Even if we appear to get away with it, it often plays on our conscience for years. And, of course, God knows exactly what we have done.

■ **PRAYER**
Lord, lead me in the ways of truth and righteousness. Amen

Song of Songs 2:11–12 (NIV)

The dove

See! The winter is past; the rains are over and gone. Flowers appear on the earth; the season of singing has come, the cooing of doves is heard in our land.

Everyone loves the spring. It is a sign of hope as the buds begin to burst on the trees and leaves and flowers start to break through the bare ground. One of the most wonderful things is the increased sound of birdsong as migrant birds are welcomed back. In Europe and the Middle East, the turtle doves return from Africa with their gentle cooing and pretty plumage. These doves mate for life. Together they build their nest, incubate their eggs and care for the young – they are truly loyal and loving.

Sadly, turtle doves, like house sparrows, have experienced a dramatic decline in the last few years and are now not far from being endangered. The reasons for the decline again include habitat loss, but also hunting. If the gentle birds that inspired the writer of the Song of Songs are to continue to be heard in the land from Israel to the UK, we need to find ways to protect and care for them. That might be by supporting a wildlife charity, making our gardens more wildlife friendly or supporting farmers as they seek to farm in ways that enable nature to flourish. Love is practical and is something we can share with God, people and all of nature.

■ **PRAYER**

Dear Lord, help us show our love for you by caring for your creation. Amen

Luke 13:34 (NIV)

The hen

'Jerusalem, Jerusalem, you who kill the prophets and stone those sent to you, how often I have longed to gather your children together, as a hen gathers her chicks under her wings, and you were not willing.'

I (Martin) lived in Jerusalem for over a year, and when I consider today's reading I imagine Jesus on his way up to the city, or maybe looking over it just as he arrives. He shows great sorrow for the people of Jerusalem, some of whom have rejected his teaching, and he longs for them to turn to him.

Jesus uses the image of a hen with her chicks, gathering them under her wings. There are many stories of mother birds doing this to protect their offspring from predators, bad weather or even fire. Not infrequently, they die themselves as a result. Of course, not long after Jesus made the statement in our reading, he died for us.

Jesus cared for the people of Jerusalem, but he also cares for us today, and we should be very grateful for that. But there is more to this. Jesus, in many respects, modelled what he expects of his followers. So we, too, should care for others who, like the people of Jerusalem in Jesus' day, have lost their way. We should all emulate the protective mother hens.

■ **PRAYER**

Lord, we thank you for your care. Show us how to care for others after your example. Amen

Absence to presence

Clare O'Driscoll

Sometimes, when I wake before the rest of my household, I creep outside with a cup of tea, my Bible tucked under one arm and a cushion under the other. There, I soak up the blissful solitude, breathing deeply of God's presence as I listen to the early birdsong.

However, while I often long for such seclusion, I'm aware that not all time alone is so relished. There have been phases in my life when I've craved the depth of connection that comes from being with others, and as such I never treat the blessing and privilege of company lightly.

It is no secret that unwanted isolation can cause both physical and mental pain. Whether through grief, broken relationships or the isolation of the lockdowns of recent years, loneliness can leave deep wounds.

Jesus, both human and divine, knew the indescribable joy of time alone with the Father, but he also knew the pain of grief and isolation. In the following reflections, we will consider how Jesus is always with us, wherever our path may lead us. He understands every challenge of absence and gently guides us into the beauty of his presence.

Mark 1:35–37 (NIV)

A quiet place

Very early in the morning, while it was still dark, Jesus got up, left the house and went off to a solitary place, where he prayed. Simon and his companions went to look for him, and when they found him, they exclaimed: 'Everyone is looking for you!'

Surrounded by the approving buzz of a crowd, many of us are tempted to find our confidence there. Jesus, however, knew this wasn't enough. He knew the superficiality and inconsistency of popularity, how it comes and goes with the wind. However nice it feels to be wanted, admiration doesn't fill the soul; only time alone with the Father does that. So Jesus found a quiet place.

When the disciples came looking for him, puzzled and possibly a little annoyed, Jesus was refreshed by his time of absence, ready to serve more people. Of course, sometimes his attempts to find solitude were curtailed by the crowd, but having made a habit of seeking God's presence, it was so second nature to him that he would always find it.

God is always with us, but coming into his presence is still a choice. When we actively and regularly choose to seek God's presence, it permeates every part of our lives, not just the deliberate alone times but the busy, chaotic times too.

■ PRAYER

Father, thank you that you see our desire to be with you and meet us wherever we are, in quiet solitude or in the busy chaos of life. Amen

2 Corinthians 12:8–9 (NIV)

A physical pain

Three times I pleaded with the Lord to take it away from me. But he said to me, 'My grace is sufficient for you, for my power is made perfect in weakness.' Therefore I will boast all the more gladly about my weaknesses, so that Christ's power may rest on me.

The pain of unchosen absence – whether grief, missing friends or feeling forgotten – can be so strong we feel it physically. Paul describes a thorn in his side. I feel it in the pit of my stomach. Either way, it's excruciating.

Like Paul, however, we can bring that brokenness before God. In his presence, our frailty has the potential to become strength. This doesn't mean everything is suddenly okay, simply that God is with us, no matter what.

We would love to think that God's presence makes up for all other absences, but we are human; the hollow pain of grief when we miss a loved one is real. God's presence is not a magic wand, taking away the pain, but a friend sitting beside us as we weep, revealing new truths and depths to us, preparing us in turn to show his presence to others.

■ PRAYER

Thank you, Father God, that when I feel weak with the pain of absence, your comforting presence can strengthen me. Please sit with me in the hurting, empty places, so that my life might show your transforming love to others. Amen

Psalm 23:3–4, 6 (NIV)

A difficult path

He guides me along the right paths for his name's sake. Even though I walk through the darkest valley, I will fear no evil, for you are with me… Surely your goodness and love will follow me all the days of my life, and I will dwell in the house of the Lord forever.

When visiting Andalucía some years back, our friends took us to a beach within a wild nature reserve. We padded along sandy scrub-lined tracks until we reached a cliff. From there, things got harder. We found ourselves battling narrow overgrown paths and tripping over tangled roots as we zigzagged towards the sea. Occasionally we lost the path completely, but seeing the glow of autumn sunlight on miles of ochre sand made it all worthwhile.

Our friends then confessed that there were far easier paths to that beach. But this particular view, this unique perspective, was only visible from our slightly awkward approach. Besides, they knew we'd appreciate the beauty more after such challenging terrain.

Some paths into God's presence are harder than others. Sometimes we seek God out of an abundance of choices. Other times we feel stripped to nothing, empty and lost. But those are the times we value his presence more than ever, often gaining a unique perspective only visible from that particular place.

■ PRAYER

Loving shepherd, when our path feels too challenging, overwhelm us with the breathtaking beauty of your presence. Amen

Mark 14:34, 40 (NIV)

Alone

'My soul is overwhelmed with sorrow to the point of death,' he said to them. 'Stay here and keep watch…' When he came back, he again found them sleeping, because their eyes were heavy.

Dusk fell, then darkness. We had been expecting my husband back from the London-to-Brighton cycle mid-afternoon, but now dinner sat stewing in a tepid oven and my overactive imagination was flying down dark lanes of despair.

Eventually he appeared and all was well; but it is hard when someone doesn't turn up. It fills us with doubt and fear.

Jesus begged his friends to stay awake with him in Gethsemane, but found himself alone. While there is often a genuine reason for absence – my husband had been waiting for a struggling teammate, Jesus' disciples were exhausted – the anxiety of being left alone is always hard.

Jesus needed his friends' support and prayers. In their absence, we hear his most anguished, brutally honest conversations with the Father. We see his deep humanity: the Jesus who wept for his friend now weeping for himself. The pain crammed into these verses is immense and if we ever doubted Jesus was human as well as divine, here we see him battle devastating isolation. Here we have a Saviour who understands the agony of absence and comforts us when we feel abandoned.

■ **PRAYER**

Jesus, thank you that you understand and are with us in the pain and doubt of loneliness. Amen

Psalm 62:7–8 (NIV)

Come as you are

My salvation and my honour depend on God; he is my mighty rock, my refuge. Trust in him at all times, you people; pour out your hearts to him, for God is our refuge.

Often in life we fall into playing the role that's required of us. We find ourselves needing to be a certain kind of person to keep things running smoothly or to manage a difficult situation. We're not deliberately faking it, but rather in small subtle ways it's easier to project a slightly 'improved' or perhaps 'protected' version of ourselves to the world. There are so few people we can trust with our innermost feelings, so few people with whom we can truly pour out our hearts.

In God's presence, however, all pretence is pointless. We don't have to list achievements or be impressive; it's futile to pretend to be an expert. We can simply be the person he created us to be – a person who has sometimes been hidden even from ourselves by our need to keep up appearances.

Spending time with God, we learn who that person really is. His presence inspires integrity deep within, teaching us to be the most honest version of ourselves. So we pour out our hearts to God or sit in comfortable silence. And the deep peace that comes from knowing we don't have to pretend becomes a gift we carry into all our interactions with others.

■ **PRAYER**

Father, may your truth-seeking presence saturate my life and relationships. Amen

John 14:27 (NIV)

A peaceful presence

'Peace I leave with you; my peace I give you. I do not give to you as the world gives. Do not let your hearts be troubled and do not be afraid.'

Near my home there's a park dotted with lakes. It is beautiful, but not perfect. A motorway cuts through the nearby forest and is faintly audible. So when I first stumbled upon the Peace Garden – a shady glen bursting with lilies and a meandering stream criss-crossed with tiny plank bridges – I sighed at its prettiness… then gave a wry laugh. Why put a Peace Garden in the noisy end of the park?

On reflection, however, perhaps it wasn't so misplaced. It is not in the tranquil parts of life that we most need peace, but in the imperfect, challenging ones, where the world's noise distracts and troubles us. A sanctuary in the storm rather than a twinkly bubble of perfection.

When Jesus promised peace, it was not in a serene, flowery garden but in a situation of unrest where the disciples would shortly face isolation and persecution. Preparing them for his imminent absence, Jesus declared peace when they would need it most. His peace is not about orchestrating perfection but about unearthing God's presence in rockier ground.

■ PRAYER

Jesus, thank you that your peace is with us in the noise and mess of life as much as in an idyllic garden. Help us to seek your presence everywhere. Amen

John 15:4–5 (NIV)

Remain in me

'Remain in me, as I also remain in you. No branch can bear fruit by itself; it must remain in the vine. Neither can you bear fruit unless you remain in me. I am the vine; you are the branches. If you remain in me and I in you, you will bear much fruit; apart from me you can do nothing.'

Hearing some rather ardent sermons when younger, I became plagued by a genuine fear that I would be 'pruned off' for not being fruitful enough. Convinced I needed to do more for God, I went to extra meetings and signed up for more duties – desperately trying to calculate how much fruit was enough – often at the expense of developing the gifts God had given me.

Sadly, much of this was not done out of love, but from fear that who I was on my own wasn't enough for God or the church. This wasn't true. It took a long time to undo that wrong idea and to realise that by simply remaining in him and being who he made me – following dreams he'd given me – I would be far more fruitful for him than any other way.

■ PRAYER

Father, thank you that our fruitfulness depends not on forced human efforts but simply on spending time in your presence, following your call. Help us to always remain in you. Amen

Joshua 1:5 (NIV)

Never abandoned

No one will be able to stand against you all the days of your life. As I was with Moses, so I will be with you; I will never leave you nor forsake you.

Sitting by the river one day, we watched intrigued and amused as a brood of ducklings swam ever closer to the shallow weir, despite their mother's noisy protestations.

Eventually, they went too far, whooshing over the edge. The mother seemed to stop and think for a moment. If a duck could sigh and roll its eyes, this one would have done both. We roared with laughter as she seemed to take a deep breath and followed her babies.

She could not leave them or abandon them; it would have been out of character, against her nature. Even in their naive foolishness, she stayed close to them and cared for them – though I'm imagining a quacky 'I told you so' as she met them at the bottom of the weir, a little shocked by the force of the water.

God does not abandon us, even when our wrong choices take us away from where we should be. He is always there, close behind us, calling us lovingly and drawing us back to himself.

■ **PRAYER**
Father, thank you for your unconditional love and presence in all situations. Help us always to choose to stay close to you. Amen

Psalm 1:3 (NIV)

Thirst-quenching presence

That person is like a tree planted by streams of water, which yields its fruit in season and whose leaf does not wither – whatever they do prospers.

When I was young, a good friend of mine lived near the river. We often played there, paddling and swinging on the lush leafy trees that grew by the water's edge. More often than not I fell in, much to the amusement of any passing boaters, and my mum often expected me to return home in borrowed clothes.

There is something so attractive and energising about being near water. Coming into God's presence is a similar experience, but without the need for so many spare clothes. Absence can feel like an arid land, making us thirsty for love, company and belonging. God's presence is refreshing and life-giving. Like water to our lives, he quenches that thirst, fulfilling our needs and bringing growth.

The best news is that we can choose not only to come close to that life-giving stream but also to be permanently planted there, our roots stretching towards him, reaching deep into the water for his sustenance.

■ **PRAYER**

Loving Father, let me be like a tree forever planted next to your streams of water so that when life feels parched and dry I can be refreshed and renewed in your presence, growing and bearing fruit for you. Amen

1 John 4:16 (NIV)

Just where we are

And so we know and rely on the love God has for us. God is love. Whoever lives in love lives in God, and God in them.

One summer's afternoon, a group of us sat in a circle outside a retreat centre, discussing questions linked to the week's theme. 'How do you find God's peace and presence?' the leader asked.

'Easy,' a young German girl said, 'I come here.' There was an awkward pause. Someone gently pointed out, 'But… you live miles away. You can't come here every time you need God's presence.'

Some places are undoubtedly special, so steeped in prayer and peace that heaven feels especially close. It is tempting to think that if we could just stay in such places forever, all would be well. But God is with us where we are right now, in the lovely and not-so-lovely parts of life, and he needs us to be signs of his loving presence in the imperfect places. As we show his love to those around us, whoever or wherever that may be, he lives in us.

Living in God's presence is not about geography, but about love. When we live lives full of his love, we live in him – always.

■ **PRAYER**

Father God, thank you that you are always present and always love us. Let me always live in your love so that I might be a tangible sign of your presence in this world. Amen

The Gift of Years

Debbie Thrower is the pioneer of BRF's Anna Chaplaincy for Older People ministry, offering spiritual care to older people, and is widely involved in training and advocacy.

Visit **annachaplaincy.org.uk** to find out more.

Debbie writes...

A woman in a care home once told a visiting young priest how she'd never perceived the presence of God, despite praying for years. It was reading a new writer to us, Clare O'Driscoll, and her description of how Jesus 'gently guides us into the beauty of his presence', which reminded me of this story, told in *School for Prayer* by Metropolitan Anthony Bloom (Libra, 1970). Do you know what the minister suggested? That the old woman should sit in her chair, facing away from dark corners, and knit for 15 minutes – without saying a word of prayer.

She did as he suggested, facing the light. She admired her nice, neat room. Then she remembered the knitting. The needles hit the armrest of her chair. She noticed her clock ticking peacefully. There was nothing to bother about... then she perceived that this silence was not simply an absence of noise: the silence had substance, a richness: 'The silence around began to come and meet the silence in me' (p. 61).

It didn't mean she stopped praying, but that she could sustain a contemplative silence for a while and then turn to vocal prayer. What a timeless secret she had learned. And the young priest who gave her this clue to such presence went on to become Russian Orthodox bishop, writer and broadcaster, Metropolitan Anthony Bloom.

Best wishes

Debbie

Meet Maggie Dodd

 Maggie Dodd was the first Anna Chaplain in the whole of Hertfordshire and in the diocese of St Albans. It's a full-time paid role, funded mainly by the Methodist Church but supported by St Peter's Anglican Church in the city. Before becoming an Anna Chaplain, Maggie worked as an illustrator and graphic designer. She lives with her retired police officer husband, two young daughters and her mother-in-law Alma, who is 90. Her own mother is living with dementia in a care home in St Albans, having been a reader in the Church of England. Her father was a vicar and Maggie has always been part of a church community. For the last 19 years, she has been a member of St Stephen's Anglican Church. We asked Maggie: What led you to Anna Chaplaincy?

I felt I was being called to some sort of ministry. I looked into ordination training in the church, but I felt that God was calling me very strongly, very tangibly, to care home ministry. I just couldn't work out where. When this job first came up and I saw the advert in the *Church Times*, I thought and prayed about it, but I wasn't sure I was being called to it at that point so I prayerfully let it go.

I was in touch with a nun who used to live next door to my mum. She wrote me a letter, encouraging me to keep searching for what I was being called to do, and said, 'If God's calling you, he won't stop calling!'

I thought I'd see if anything inspired me, picked up the *Church Times*, which had arrived that day, and the advert was there again – they hadn't filled the position first time round. So I thought, 'Okay Lord, I get the message!' So I applied, was interviewed and was lucky enough to be offered the job, and I was thrilled about it.

How much were you influenced by your closeness to your mum and to your mother-in-law?

Very much so. Mum's dementia was diagnosed about three or so years ago, but my father died about seven years ago. Even then, I think he realised that Mum wasn't as sharp as she used to be and was missing things. When he died, it became obvious that she really couldn't manage on her own without Dad.

We took the decision to move Mum closer to me, but when she moved there were things that I felt could have been done better. She kind of fell through a gap. When she moved into the care home, her faith wasn't really considered and nurtured, and there wasn't an obvious contact to make there. It felt as if that very important part of her life wasn't actively welcomed and supported. So I started to do things at her care home – simple activities with hymns and crafts. That obviously influenced my feeling towards older people's ministry and how there were gaps that needed to be linked up in the way that Anna Chaplains can do: helping to join up church communities with care home communities.

There's a particular need for that when so many older people move away from their own communities to a care home or sheltered housing near their children. We have to be very aware of that loss and help them engage with and become part of a new church community so they don't lose everything just because it's the best thing for them to be closer to family.

And I live with my mother-in-law, so I know the challenges she faces, watching her independence and mobility diminish and being very aware of what she misses, even though she's mentally very sharp. She's not a regular churchgoer, but there's a spirituality in helping people feel cared for, welcomed, listened to and included. It's so important to help people, whatever their faith, feel part of the community and engaged in local activities and to feel valued for who they are.

How important is the Anna Chaplain network to you?

It's wonderful! It's such a great source of encouragement and shared experience. Everyone I've met within the network has been so open and willing to share their experience, knowledge and ideas. To know that it's not just you on your own, and if you get stuck there's always someone to help, is hugely important.

The website and the blog are so up to date that if I meet someone and they're interested in finding out more I always direct them to the website. There's so much good information there that it does a lot of my work for me.

What would you say to encourage others to get involved with Anna Chaplaincy?

If people are interested in other people's stories, and in caring for a part of society that gets overlooked so often, then it's a wonderfully rewarding ministry to get involved in. Older people have so much to offer and have lived such full lives. If, maybe, they don't remember those lives so well any more, you could help them find a path back to some of those memories and experiences.

And you could help to ease the pressure on families and carers, and people who worry about their frail mums and dads who they can't get to see as much as they'd like. If they know someone is going in to see them and give them a cup of tea and have a chat, it means so much. You can make a huge difference in a small way!

Third Sunday after Easter

Victoria Field is a writer, poetry therapist and researcher. Her recent books are a poetry collection, *A Speech of Birds*, and a memoir of pilgrimage and marriage, *Baggage: A book of leavings*, both published by Francis Boutle. She was named in *Poetry Review* as a pioneer in the use of poetry and healing and has a particular interest in public libraries and people living with dementia. Her doctoral research at Canterbury Christ Church University is on narratives of transformation and pilgrimage. See **thepoetrypractice.co.uk**.

Victoria's poem 'Third Sunday after Easter' was written during her time as artist-in-residence at Truro Cathedral, beginning in Advent 2005.

Third Sunday after Easter

The end of April is yellow and white –
earth all three-cornered garlic and celandines.

The beginning of May is white and yellow –
every hillside clouded by blackthorn and gorse.

The end of April is walls of scent, doors open
silently into summer. The beginning of May

is carpets of sea, windows to wide horizons
and gates ajar. Walking between these months

is a path balancing land and water, held
in the arms of new grass, always heading west.

Something's begun – white as new linen
yellow as remembered sun.

From *Many Waters* by Victoria Field (Fal Publications, 2006).
Used with kind permission.

Lessons from the Camino – Angela Lucas

We first met Angela Lucas in these pages exactly a year ago. In that interview she talked about her life and her book, *How to be a SuperAger: Living life to the max in your 50s, 60s and beyond* (Panoma Press, 2018). In her book, she described how she'd been challenged to walk 100 kilometres (62 miles) of the Camino – the ancient pilgrim route to Santiago de Compostela – at the age of 82. The last chapter is called 'Wrapping up the Camino experience' and Angela has kindly given us permission to print an edited extract here.

My Camino adventure echoed life. Life has diverse moments, some of them terribly sad or difficult, many of them incredibly enriching and beautiful. My Camino neared its end as we entered the ancient Santiago square with its imposing cathedral. My daughter and I punched the air and jumped as high as our backpacks would allow, with the utter exuberance of accomplishment.

Then we entered the cathedral itself. This was a moment of stillness and joy as we joined hundreds of others sitting in the coolness of the building to be still and to reflect that in spite of the mud and heat, we did it. Not that we thought this was the end, but rather it was the onward process of thinking, if I could do this, then what else can I do?

But in that moment of stillness there was another, deeper reflection. Along the way we had walked alongside other *peregrinos* (pilgrims), and in that rarefied atmosphere far away from the details of home life, people would share their stories. People had hiked their Caminos for various reasons, but usually the stories they told were of pain and of loss.

On arrival in Santiago and entering the cathedral for the midday Pilgrim's Mass, a whole new meaning was perceived in the sharing of the Eucharist… and the Peace.

To be honoured with these rituals among people whom we met on the journey, whose stories of pain, loss and bewilderment had been shared as they walked: these things gave a very different emphasis to the traditional theology. It is unlikely I shall ever sit comfortably on a church pew again without remembering how deep the unity of sharing our faith can really go.

I looked around me and saw the fine young Italian man who, having lost his faith in God, was challenged by his priest to go on the Camino – taking nothing at all with him, not even money. He told us his story, how he found God to be real in the lives of people he had met on his pilgrimage. On a further aisle, sitting huddled up with her grief, was a young German woman whose husband had walked out on her. I hugged the American man who, finding the pilgrimage too tough, had wanted to quit, but there he was standing tall and so pleased to have completed his challenge.

The cathedral filled with rising clouds of incense from the great brass *Botafumeiro* – swung low past our shoulders by several priests – and it seemed to me that the incense echoed the holiness of prayer.

The white smoke wrapped itself around all these people, from many nations and with many complicated sorrows, before rising higher and higher, taking up their sadness and their joys to hold in the presence of the living God. This made the pilgrimage complete.

You may not be able to, or wish to, go hiking the Camino. But within your own parameters, it might still be possible to carve out for yourself that amazing thing called living; as far as possible live your dreams. Whatever your adventure or choice will be, I wish you well.

Best wishes
Angela

Everyday parables

Derek Morgan

I don't know about you, but I sometimes find it difficult to under-stand a new concept or idea, even if the other person repeats the explanation over and over again. However, once they can give me an example using something I already know well and relate it to this new thing, it all clicks into place and becomes clear.

The New Testament tells us that when Jesus walked the earth and talked to both his disciples and the crowds, he would often talk in parables. He would use an object or a situation that everyone knew well and use it to explain a deeper spiritual meaning.

You could say that a parable is an earthly story with a heavenly mean-ing or that it illustrates the invisible – spiritual – world by using an analogy from the visible – natural – world. Jesus was the master story-teller and he knew that people would remember what he said for much longer if he spoke using parables.

In this series of reflections, I've used everyday objects that I think you will know well and have used them to illustrate a biblical truth. My prayer is that many of these will strike a chord and will really bless you.

2 Corinthians 2:15 (NKJV)

Heaven scent

For we are to God the fragrance of Christ among those who are being saved and among those who are perishing.

I'm one of those men who still likes to use a bit of aftershave, ideally with the right fragrance for the occasion. Some while ago, I bought some random aftershave and I found I really liked it. It became one of my favourites, until one day I happened to read the label and realised it was called 'Pagan Man'. This made me stop and wonder as to what impact my 'fragrance' was having on those around me.

Does my life give off the beautiful fragrance of Christ? Do the people I come into contact with see the kindness, humility, gentleness and patience that Paul mentions in his letter to the Colossians? Or, dare I say it, does the 'Pagan Man' show through? Am I speaking and acting in a way that is contrary to those things that Paul says?

A few years ago, a British songwriter called Graham Kendrick wrote a song entitled 'May the fragrance'. These wonderful lyrics, which ask Jesus' beauty and fragrance to fill our lives, are words to live up to, don't you think?

■ **PRAYER**

Dear Lord, we want to be your fragrance to those around us. Fill us with your Holy Spirit so that we can be the kind of people you intend us to be. Amen

Revelation 3:20 (NLT)

Man's best friend

'Look! I [Jesus], stand at the door and knock. If you hear my voice and open the door, I will come in, and we will share a meal together as friends.'

I wonder whether you have a pet dog or if you once had a dog? If so, you will know just how much of a friend and loyal companion they can be. There are no prizes for guessing who gets tired first when playing fetch with that ball. And how often have you felt you would really like some comfort or cheering up, and, just when you need them, there they are with a waggy tail and a ready nuzzle.

As today's verse says, Jesus wants to come in and be part of our lives, and he even uses the word 'friend' to indicate just how close a relationship he wants to have with us. There's a lovely hymn entitled 'What a friend we have in Jesus'. Whether our issue is loneliness, discouragement, grief, pain or anything else, we can, and should, pray about it and ask for the Lord's help to see us through it. Jesus is right there now, just waiting for you to talk to him.

■ **PRAYER**

Lord God, you know us better than we know ourselves. Thank you that you are always there for us and are only a prayer away. Amen

1 Peter 4:10 (NLT)

The wind of the Spirit

God has given each of you a gift from his great variety of spiritual gifts. Use them well to serve one another.

I have always enjoyed travelling and I used to collect souvenirs of places that particularly appealed to me. Many years ago, while out exploring a new area, I wandered into a shop of locally made handicrafts. My eye was taken by a beautifully made wind chime. I tried it in the shop and the sound was as beautiful as the craftmanship, so I bought it. I took it home and proudly hung it in the lounge of my house. For quite a while, I took great pleasure in looking at the wind chime, but eventually it became largely ignored and just gathered dust.

Several years later, I realised that the person who made it never intended that wind chime to be hung indoors. That wind chime was designed to be outside with the wind blowing through it, so that the beautiful music could be heard by those around.

Similarly, when we know Jesus, the wind of his Holy Spirit should blow through us and we should make a beautiful impact on those around us. Although our God-given abilities and gifts may not be what they were, there will always be something we can do to bless those around us.

■ PRAYER

Dear Lord, as we become less able to serve you as we once did, help us still to be a beautiful witness for you. Amen

Romans 12:2a (NLT)

What a transformation

Don't copy the behaviour and customs of this world, but let God transform you into a new person by changing the way you think.

When my son was quite small, he had a couple of toy cars called Transformers. They were very cleverly designed so that by bending or twisting bits of the car, it was 'transformed' into a robot with arms, legs and head. Hours of fun for both of us.

God, the greatest designer of them all, wants to transform us too. Not by bending and twisting us into different shapes, fortunately, but, as our Bible passage above tells us, through the work of the Holy Spirit in our lives. We just need to commit ourselves to honouring Jesus in whatever way we can.

Even better, God doesn't stop there. In the letter that Paul wrote to the church in Corinth, he explains how God has perfect plans for his children, saying, 'Our earthly bodies, the ones we have now that can die, must be transformed into heavenly bodies that cannot perish but will live forever' (1 Corinthians 15:53, TLB). How wonderful to look forward to a time when the aches, pains and disabilities of our tired old bodies will be a thing of the past. We will be with God and have new bodies that will never wear out. I can't wait.

■ **PRAYER**

Dear Lord, please keep on transforming us into your likeness. Amen

Isaiah 40:31 (ESV)

Sea soaring

But they who wait for the Lord shall renew their strength; they shall mount up with wings like eagles; they shall run and not be weary; they shall walk and not faint.

I'm blessed to live overlooking the sea, and I'm used to seeing seagulls flapping around the area. Recently, on a particularly windy day when not many birds were about, I spotted one lone seagull high up in the sky soaring around gracefully with wings outstretched. It reminded me of the Bible passage above, which is actually just one of many passages about eagles.

Eagles are the most majestic and powerful of birds, and it is easy to imagine why they were selected. For me, however, that sight of the seagull soaring was a particularly special moment, as it showed a very ordinary bird being treated in the same way. It helped me to see that God doesn't just come to the aid of special people but he is equally interested in ordinary people.

If any of us are feeling down, depressed or forgotten, we can cry out to God and he will come alongside and lift us up, whoever we are. God said through Isaiah, 'Don't be afraid, for I am with you. Don't be discouraged, for I am your God. I will strengthen you and help you. I will hold you up' (Isaiah 41:10, NLT).

■ **PRAYER**
Gracious Lord, thank you that you hear us when we cry out to you.
Amen

Philippians 4:6 (NLT)

Mastering that juggling act

Don't worry about anything; instead, pray about everything. Tell God what you need, and thank him for all he has done.

Many years ago I decided I wanted to learn something new and, for whatever reason, I chose juggling. After many hours of chasing those stupid balls around the floor, first one ball, then two, I finally managed to keep three balls going in the air at the same time.

Juggling three balls is a lot easier than trying to juggle a stressful job, a family and a mortgage – or perhaps these days it is more likely to be failing health, an inadequate pension and looking after the grand-children. However, I learnt that when juggling balls, you don't actually look at the balls, but you look through and beyond them. Not only that, but I realised that I could apply the same lesson to life's problems too.

When trying to juggle these problems, don't get totally stressed by each one, but look through and beyond them to see ways that you can bring Jesus into the situation.

Praying about problems, giving them to Jesus, asking him for help, strength, peace, endurance, patience, creativity or whatever it is you need, will make the task of juggling them much easier. Asking him to take our anxiety and lift the burden brings a wonderful peace.

■ PRAYER

Dear Lord, thank you that we can cast all our cares on you, because we know you care for us. Amen

1 Samuel 16:7b (NKJV)

You are unique

For the Lord does not see as man sees; for man looks at the outward appearance, but the Lord looks at the heart.

If you have read any murder mystery books or watched any detective programmes on television, I'm fairly certain you will be familiar with that moment near the end when the fingerprints of the suspect are matched with those on the murder weapon. Fingerprints have been used to solve crimes for more than 100 years, because every one of us leaves a unique mark behind. Even identical twins, with identical DNA, have different fingerprints. No one else has the same hoops, whirls and ridges that you do.

The Bible tells us that God sees each of us as unique individuals but, as the verse above says, God doesn't look at our fingerprints to tell who we are. He looks at our hearts.

The big question is: what will God see when he looks at our hearts? The worst-case scenario, as Mark's gospel tells us, is that he will see evil thoughts, theft, murder, greed, wickedness, deceit, lustful desires, envy, etc. (Mark 7:21–22) and we really don't want those in our hearts.

Fortunately, reading the Bible and praying can change our hearts. Jesus says, 'Blessed are the pure in heart, for they shall see God' (Matthew 5:8, NIV). Can you imagine how wonderful that will be?

■ PRAYER

Loving Lord, create in me a clean heart and renew a right spirit within me. Amen

2 Timothy 3:16a (NLT)

The hidden truth

All Scripture is inspired by God and is useful to teach us what is true.

If you cast your mind back to your younger days, do you remember having a reel-to-reel tape player or maybe a portable cassette tape recorder? I can still recall the days when something went wrong with the tape player and that shiny brown tape got itself totally tangled up in the mechanism – very frustrating. It's an interesting truth that the brown tape looks very ordinary but it contains far more than is visible to the human eye. You need the tape machine in order to reveal the words or music hidden in the tape.

It's a similar situation with the Bible. You can read it as a kind of historical storybook but, just like the tape, it contains far more than that. God has given us the Holy Spirit to reveal more than just the words written on the page. In Paul's letters to Timothy, he says God can 'speak' to us through what we read, showing us a deeper meaning or providing guidance or comfort. We just need to be patient and be open.

Archaeology keeps on providing proof of the Bible's authenticity, so when we read 'whoever believes in him [Jesus] will not perish but have eternal life' (John 3:16, NIV), we know we can take that as the gospel truth.

■ PRAYER

Dear Lord, thank you for your sacrifice and your gift of eternal life. Amen

Proverbs 3:5–6 (GNT)

It's all a matter of balance

Trust in the Lord with all your heart. Never rely on what you think you know. Remember the Lord in everything you do, and he will show you the right way.

Do you remember when you learnt how to ride a bicycle? It may have been some time ago, but you may still remember finding your balance and that wonderful feeling of freedom. Maybe you still ride today (good for you!).

It's an interesting fact of science that something that is impossible when stationary – such as balancing on a bike – becomes a world of possibilities when it has forward momentum.

The Christian life is often referred to as a journey, and we could stretch the analogy to a journey on a bike. While we are constantly moving forward, seeking to learn more from the Bible, deepening our relationship with God and being guided by the Holy Spirit, Jesus can take us to places we never imagined.

However, if we stop moving forward in these ways, if we stop reading the Bible and talking to God, our bike slows down and before long we will lose our balance and eventually fall off. How much better to keep peddling and keep going to new places with God.

■ PRAYER

Heavenly Father, help us always to seek you, even when things of the world seem to hold us back. Amen

Deuteronomy 31:8a (NLT)

Don't be sad

Do not be afraid or discouraged, for the Lord will personally go ahead of you. He will be with you.

Are you one of those people who finds that for some reason, during the winter season, you seem to lose interest in everyday things and you feel lethargic and sleepy? It is said that such feelings could be an indication of Seasonal Affective Disorder. You can even buy SAD lamps for your house that are extra bright and mimic summer sunshine, and if you sit by them for some time they may make you feel better. That cure for 'SAD-ness' may sound too good to be true, but what we do know to be true is what the Bible says to us about feeling sad.

Just look at the following examples: Jesus says, 'Don't let your hearts be troubled; trust in God, and trust also in me' (John 14:1); 'The Lord is close to the brokenhearted' (Psalm 34:18); 'Give all your worries and cares to God, for he cares about you' (1 Peter 5:7).

There are many reasons why we may feel sad. Sometimes there is a really good explanation for it, but other times we can feel sad for no particular reason at all. If you are feeling sad at the moment, please talk to Jesus about it. He is waiting to help you.

■ **PRAYER**

Dear Lord, revive our hearts by the refreshing of your Holy Spirit and give us your perfect peace. Amen

Hymns of hope

Emlyn Williams

Singing can bring hope in dark times. African American slaves expressed their heavenly hope as they sang spirituals in the plantations of the American South. Long before that, Paul and Silas sang hymns in prison (Acts 16:25). And today, music is still a powerful aid for enduring hardship. One of the first responses to the Covid-19 pandemic lockdowns was an outbreak of online choirs and singing.

This series of reflections links together well-known hymns and Bible passages to remind us of the hope that we have. Sometimes they include a little of the story or background to the hymn. Some of the Bible passages are directly referred to in the hymn; others bring to the hymn a wider perspective from the scriptures.

Space limitations mean that we have not been able to print all the words of the hymns. So, if you have a hymn book, keep it to hand while you read. Alternatively, you'll be able to find the words of hymns on sites such as **hymnary.org**. We have included a simple link to You-Tube videos of the hymn and many of them have the words as well as the sound. So why not sing along while you read and pray?

John 14:27 (NIV)

Peace like a river

Peace I leave with you; my peace I give you. I do not give to you as the world gives. Do not let your hearts be troubled and do not be afraid.

> *When peace like a river attendeth my way,*
> *when sorrows like sea billows roll;*
> *whatever my lot, thou hast taught me to say,*
> *'It is well, it is well with my soul.'*

Horatio Spafford (1828–88), **youtu.be/AHe_qmo3gX4**

One morning, when I was under great stress, I woke up humming a hymn about peace. At that moment, I had an overwhelming sense of peace, as though Jesus was speaking to me as he did here to the disciples. Circumstances hadn't changed, but I went into that day with a sense of calm and peace. The peace Jesus offers is no ordinary peace. It is his peace, tried and tested. It surpasses all understanding (Philippians 4:7, NRSV).

This hymn was written in tragic circumstances. Horatio Spafford was an American lawyer, who, having lost his son in a house fire, went on to lose most of his wealth in an economic downturn in 1873. He had planned to visit England with his family, but had last-minute business to attend to and sent them on ahead of him. In a dreadful mid-Atlantic accident, his four daughters were lost at sea. On the voyage to meet his wife, as his ship passed the spot where his daughters had drowned, he was inspired to write the words of this well-loved hymn.

■ PRAYER

Lord Jesus, please give that peace which you have promised to those I know and love, today. Amen

Hebrews 6:18b–19 (NIV)

An anchor in the storm

We who have fled to take hold of the hope set before us may be greatly encouraged. We have this hope as an anchor for the soul, firm and secure.

We have an anchor that keeps the soul
steadfast and sure while the billows roll;
fastened to the Rock which cannot move,
grounded firm and deep in the Saviour's love!

Priscilla J. Owens (1829–1907), **youtu.be/F9aLhTHmuTg**

I've just seen a 1960s Boys' Brigade hat on eBay, exactly like the one I used to wear as a boy. I'm sure it's much more expensive now than mine was. But it brought back lots of memories, especially the emblem, an anchor and the motto, 'Sure and Steadfast'. Both of them refer to today's Bible reading. What a great passage for the world's first uniformed voluntary youth organisation.

But the verse – and the motto – are much more than an encouragement to safety and solidity. The 'hope set before us' (v. 18), the hope that is 'an anchor for the soul' (v. 19) is the certainty that God will keep his promises. So when the storms of life hit us, when we wonder whether we can hang on any longer, we can know that we are secure. Why? Because we are fastened to Jesus, 'the Rock which cannot move'. In the darkest days, a hymn of hope like this one reminds us of where our security lies.

■ **PRAYER**
Pray for anyone you know – including yourself – who needs the reassurance that they are anchored to a rock which cannot move.

Psalm 23:1–2, 4 (NIV, abridged)

Unfailing goodness

The Lord is my shepherd, I lack nothing. He makes me lie down in green pastures, he leads me beside quiet waters... Even though I walk through the darkest valley, I will fear no evil, for you are with me.

The King of love my shepherd is,
whose goodness faileth never.
I nothing lack if I am his,
and he is mine forever.

H.W. Baker (1821–77), **youtu.be/zNnuM1Z8FzI**

Is there a better-known psalm than this one? I doubt it. It's a psalm for everyone. Green pastures (v. 2) and dark valleys (v. 4) capture the ups and downs of our experience of life. No wonder this hymn is among the most popular ones for both weddings and funerals.

David the shepherd was writing from personal experience, both of being a shepherd and also of needing a shepherd. When we're in the dark valleys of life, we need the presence of the shepherd. But we also need the hope that the good shepherd (see John 10:11) will lead us to green pasture for rest and refreshment.

David's hope was resourced by his past experience of God. Taking time to recall God's faithfulness in the past strengthens our hope for the future. Why not do that now? A friend once said to me in a dark time, 'God has never let you down, has he? So why would you expect him to be different now?'

■ **PRAYER**

Good shepherd, be with me and those I love throughout today to guide, protect and feed. Amen

Matthew 7:24–25 (NIV)

A firm foundation

'Therefore everyone who hears these words of mine and puts them into practice is like a wise man who built his house on the rock. The rain came down, the streams rose, and the winds blew and beat against that house; yet it did not fall, because it had its foundation on the rock.'

How firm a foundation, ye saints of the Lord,
is laid for your faith in his excellent Word!
What more can he say than to you he has said,
you who unto Jesus for refuge have fled?

Anonymous (1787), **youtu.be/yqfvlmePJO4**

A major way in which God brings us hope is through the Bible. Which Bible verses have helped you in the past? Try to recall some of them now. Like squirrels storing away food for the winter, reading, and memorising if we can, prepares us in advance. But as Jesus said, we need to live his words as well as reading them (v. 24).

No one is absolutely certain who wrote this great hymn. The first publication in 1787 gave the author's name as just 'K–', which leaves all sorts of possibilities. The words of the hymn exemplify its teaching about the foundation of God's word. It contains many references to Bible passages such as 'Fear not, for I am with you' (Isaiah 41:10, ESV). Look up the rest of the hymn and see how many others you can find.

■ PRAYER

Thank you, Lord, for the Bible and the strength and hope it brings. Help me get to know it better and live it out daily.

Psalm 46:1–2, 10 (NIV)

Be still

God is our refuge and strength, an ever-present help in trouble. Therefore we will not fear, though the earth give way and the mountains fall into the heart of the sea... He says, 'Be still, and know that I am God; I will be exalted among the nations, I will be exalted in the earth.'

> *Be still, my soul! for God will undertake*
> *to guide the future surely as the past.*
> *Your hope, your confidence, let nothing shake;*
> *all now mysterious shall be clear at last.*
> *Be still, my soul! the waves and winds still know*
> *the voice that calmed their fury long ago.*
>
> Kathrina von Schlegel (1697–1797), translated by Jane Borthwick (1813–97),
> **youtu.be/snGEoVfUGuQ**

As I started to write this, I received an email from a friend who had just received bad news. Both the psalm and the hymn seemed so relevant. Having hope in hard times doesn't mean that everything will turn out as we want. But it does mean that God is there with us whatever happens, even if the outcome is the worst we can imagine. Things are not out of his control.

The question 'Why?' is often on our lips at times like this. In my experience, most of the time we don't have an answer. But this hymn holds out the hope that whether we know it now or not, eventually things will be clearer: 'all now mysterious shall be clear at last'.

■ PRAYER

Thank you, Lord, that we can be assured that you will 'guide the future surely as the past'. Please calm the storms of our lives today. Amen

1 Timothy 6:15–16 (NIV)

Immortal, invisible

God, the blessed and only Ruler, the King of kings and Lord of lords, who alone is immortal and who lives in unapproachable light, whom no one has seen or can see. To him be honour and might forever. Amen.

Immortal, invisible, God only wise,
in light inaccessible, hid from our eyes,
most blessed, most glorious, the Ancient of Days,
almighty, victorious, thy great name we praise.
Unresting, unhasting, and silent as light,
nor wanting, nor wasting, thou rulest in might,
thy justice like mountains high soaring above
thy clouds, which are fountains of goodness and love.

Walter C. Smith (1824–1908), **youtu.be/AZA94ncis0g**

It's good that we can know God as our close heavenly Father. But in the dark days of our lives, we face the mystery of the invisible God. Look at the adjectives in the first verse: immortal, invisible, wise, inaccessible, hid, blessed, glorious, almighty, victorious. When things in our lives are serious, don't we need to know that God is like this?

Perhaps we are sometimes in danger of failing to recognise the power and majesty of God. At times, we may treat him like just another friend. But while he is a friend, he is no ordinary friend. Walter C. Smith, who wrote this hymn, took God very seriously. The hymn took almost 40 years to write as he struggled to express what is inexpressible.

■ PRAYER

As you come to God in prayer, take time to reflect on the mystery of a God 'whom no one has seen' (v. 16), yet who revealed himself to us in Jesus.

Isaiah 55:8–9 (NIV)

God's mysterious ways

'For my thoughts are not your thoughts, neither are your ways my ways,' declares the Lord. 'As the heavens are higher than the earth, so are my ways higher than your ways and my thoughts than your thoughts.'

God moves in a mysterious way his wonders to perform.
He plants his footsteps in the sea and rides upon the storm.
You fearful saints, fresh courage take; the clouds you so much
  dread
Are big with mercy and shall break in blessings on your head.

William Cowper (1731–1800), **youtu.be/9MgbVoyPWTo**

Sometimes the words of a hymn pass into the language as a saying detached from the hymn. This is a good example. How often have you heard someone say 'God moves in a mysterious way' in response to something puzzling? Said sincerely, however, it's a great expression of faith.

This hymn emerged from William Cowper's lifelong and unresolved struggle with mental illness and depression. In tough times, it's tempting to tell God what he should do. But while God's ways and plans are often clear, sometimes they are mysterious. The point in both the Bible verse and the hymn is that even when things don't work out as we hope or expect, we can trust that God knows what he is doing. Look back over your life and try to think of times when God's mysteries have turned out to be blessings.

■ **PRAYER**

Father God, thank you for the security that comes from knowing that you are both powerful and good. Amen

James 4:7–8, 10 (NIV)

Nearer to thee

Submit yourselves, then, to God. Resist the devil, and he will flee from you. Come near to God and he will come near to you… Humble yourselves before the Lord, and he will lift you up.

> *Nearer, my God, to thee, nearer to thee!*
> *E'en though it be a cross that raiseth me,*
> *still all my song shall be,*
> *nearer, my God, to thee;*
> *nearer, my God, to thee, nearer to thee!*
>
> Sarah F. Adams (1805–48), **youtu.be/rwLl5nY5WPl**

According to the film, the band on the Titanic played this hymn as the ship went down. Well, the jury is out on whether it actually did, but it would have been a great choice. For many people, times of crisis drive them nearer to God. The hymn is based on Jacob's famous dream (Genesis 28:10–22). Running away from home to a foreign country, Jacob slept under the stars and dreamed of angels going up and down a stairway between heaven and earth.

In the dream God showed Jacob another dimension to reality. Though he couldn't see them outside the dream, angels were at work and God was present. Another verse of the hymn says, 'There let the way appear, steps unto heaven / all that thou sendest me, in mercy given / angels to beckon me.' However difficult our situation, God and his angels are active and nearer than we realise. We are not alone in our pain.

■ **PRAYER**

Take a little time to be still before God and ask him to come near to you as he has promised.

Psalm 18:1–3 (NIV)

Rock of ages

I love you, Lord, my strength. The Lord is my rock, my fortress and my deliverer; my God is my rock, in whom I take refuge, my shield and the horn of my salvation, my stronghold. I called to the Lord, who is worthy of praise, and I have been saved from my enemies.

Rock of Ages, cleft for me,
let me hide myself in thee;
let the water and the blood,
from thy riven side which flowed,
be of sin the double cure;
cleanse me from its guilt and power.

Augustus Toplady (1740–78), **youtu.be/hS0uh_6ctG4**

In a gorge in the Mendip hills in Somerset is a rock marked 'Rock of Ages'. Legend has it that Augustus Toplady sheltered there during a storm and was inspired to write this hymn. Its focus is on Christ as our protector, who can deal with our sin and bring us to God.

Whether the story of Toplady sheltering there is true or not, the image of a rock is a powerful reminder, bringing hope in times of difficulty. Four times in this psalm (vv. 2, 31, 46) David refers to God as a rock, portraying him as much more than just a shelter from a storm. He was his fortress, the deliverer from his enemies. He was his refuge and shield, bringing shade from the fierce heat of the desert. How might it help you today to remember that God is your rock?

■ **PRAYER**

Rock of Ages, cleft for me, let me hide myself in thee. Amen

Philippians 4:6–7 (NIV)

What a friend we have in Jesus

Do not be anxious about anything, but in every situation, by prayer and petition, with thanksgiving, present your requests to God. And the peace of God, which transcends all understanding, will guard your hearts and your minds in Christ Jesus.

What a friend we have in Jesus,
all our sins and griefs to bear!
What a privilege to carry
everything to God in prayer!
O what peace we often forfeit,
O what needless pain we bear,
all because we do not carry
everything to God in prayer!

Joseph Scriven (1819–86), **youtu.be/Prthhmly0Gg**

Anxiety is a perfectly understandable human response which we all experience at times. But what do we do with it? The simple – but not simplistic – answer of this hymn is what Paul told the Philippians: take it to God in prayer (v. 6).

This well-loved hymn comes out of experience of great pain and suffering. Joseph Scriven was an Irish immigrant to Canada. In 1844, he had the shattering experience of his fiancée dying in a drowning accident on the eve of their wedding. Tragically, history repeated itself when he was again engaged to be married and his new wife-to-be also died after a short illness. In 1855, when he heard that his mother at home in Ireland was very ill, he wrote this hymn to let her know what Jesus meant to him.

■ PRAYER

Father God, I lay before you all the things which are making me anxious. May I know your peace today. Amen

One size fits all?

For just as the body is one and has many members, and all the members of the body, though many, are one body, so it is with Christ. For in one Spirit we were all baptised into one body.

2 CORINTHIANS 12:12 (ESV)

Trying to make something that works for everyone is an immensely difficult task – ask anyone who has ever tried to plan a group holiday! Throw that out to the entire world – we know that people are wonderfully and remarkably different and we change so much throughout our lives as well. From babies to children to adults to older people, everyone is spectacularly unique.

Our mission as a charity is to encourage all people of all ages to grow in their faith. We share the message of God's love for the world in many different ways, because we know that a one-size-fits-all approach doesn't work with the profoundly varied world our God created.

From our Living Faith team creating Bible reading notes for individuals, like the ones you are holding now, to our Parenting for Faith team working to empower parents to raise God-connected children and teenagers. From our Messy Church team resourcing and equipping leaders to run church that reaches out to families to our Anna Chaplaincy team sustaining those working with older people, combatting loneliness and bringing comfort.

We're always looking for new ways to help people grow in faith as well as ways to reach more people with the things we do. Our work is only possible because of generous donations from individuals, charitable trusts and gifts in wills. If you would like to help us make what we do possible through a regular gift, find out how to give at **brf.org. uk/friends** or get in touch with our fundraising team on 01235 462305 or via **giving@brf.org.uk**.

Your prayers, as ever, are hugely appreciated.

Judith Moore
Fundraising development officer

Grief Notes
Walking through loss
The first year after bereavement

Tony Horsfall

In *Grief Notes* Tony Horsfall charts the first year of his grief journey since the death of his wife from cancer. Month by month he tells the unfolding story of walking with and through loss, weaving this together with biblical teaching on grief and insights gained from grief counselling. With a poignant mix of honesty and humour, Tony shares the challenges of rebuilding his life and reflects on how he has seen God meet his needs as he wrestled with grieving in a time of lockdown and pandemic.

Grief Notes: Walking through loss
The first year after bereavement
Tony Horsfall
978 1 80039 126 0 £8.99
brfonline.org.uk

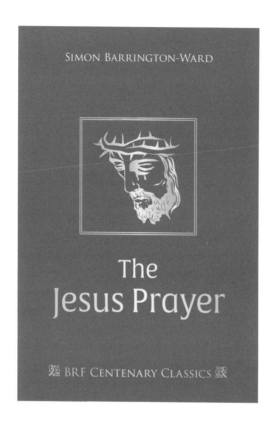

'Lord Jesus Christ, Son of God, have mercy on me.' This ancient prayer has been known and loved by generations of Christians for hundreds of years. It is a way of entering into the river of prayer which flows from the heart of God: the prayer of God himself, as Jesus continually prays for his people and for the world he loves. Simon Barrington-Ward teaches us how to use the Jesus Prayer as a devotional practice, and opens up the Bible passages that are crucial to understanding it.

The Jesus Prayer
BRF Centenary Classics
Simon Barrington-Ward
978 1 80039 087 4 £14.99
brfonline.org.uk

To order

Online: **brfonline.org.uk**
Telephone: +44 (0)1865 319700
Mon–Fri 9.30–17.00
Post: complete this form and send to the address below

Delivery times within the UK are normally 15 working days. Prices are correct at the time of going to press but may change without prior notice.

Title	Issue*	Price	Qty	Total
Grief Notes: Walking through loss		£8.99		
The Jesus Prayer		£14.99		
Bible Reflections for Older People (single copy)	May–Aug 2022	£5.35		
Bible Reflections for Older People (single copy)	Sep–Dec 2022	£5.35		

POSTAGE AND PACKING CHARGES			
Order value	UK	Europe	Rest of world
Under £7.00	£2.00	Available on request	Available on request
£7.00–£29.99	£3.00		
£30.00 and over	FREE		

Total value of books	
Donation	
Postage and packing	
Total for this order	

Please complete in BLOCK CAPITALS

Title .... First name/initials .... Surname ....

Address ....

.... Postcode ....

Acc. No. .... Telephone ....

Email ....

Method of payment

❑ Cheque (made payable to BRF) ❑ MasterCard / Visa

Card no. ☐☐☐☐ ☐☐☐☐ ☐☐☐☐ ☐☐☐☐

Expires end ☐☐ ☐☐ Security code ☐☐☐ Last 3 digits on the reverse of the card

Please return this form to:

BRF, 15 The Chambers, Vineyard, Abingdon OX14 3FE | **enquiries@brf.org.uk**
For terms and cancellation information, please visit **brfonline.org.uk/terms**.

Bible Reading Fellowship is a charity (233280) and company limited by guarantee (301324), registered in England and Wales

BIBLE REFLECTIONS FOR OLDER PEOPLE **GROUP SUBSCRIPTION FORM**

> All our Bible reading notes can be ordered online
> by visiting **brfonline.org.uk/subscriptions**

The group subscription rate for *Bible Reflections for Older People* will be £16.05 per person until April 2023.

☐ I would like to take out a group subscription for .... (*quantity*) copies.

☐ Please start my order with the September 2022 / January 2023 / May 2023* issue.
   (*delete as appropriate*)

Please do not send any money with your order. Send your order to BRF and we will send you an invoice.

Name and address of the person organising the group subscription:

Title .... First name/initials .... Surname ....

Address ....

.... Postcode ....

Telephone .... Email ....

Church ....

Name and address of the person paying the invoice if the invoice needs to be sent directly to them:

Title .... First name/initials .... Surname ....

Address ....

.... Postcode ....

Telephone .... Email ....

Please return this form to:
BRF, 15 The Chambers, Vineyard, Abingdon OX14 3FE | **enquiries@brf.org.uk**
For terms and cancellation information, please visit **brfonline.org.uk/terms**.

Bible Reading Fellowship is a charity (233280) and company limited by guarantee (301324), registered in England and Wales

> To order online, please visit **brfonline.org.uk/subscriptions**

☐ I would like to take out a subscription (*complete your name and address details only once*)
☐ I would like to give a gift subscription (*please provide both names and addresses*)

Title .... First name/initials .... Surname..

Address...

.... Postcode ....

Telephone .... Email ....

Gift subscription name ....

Gift subscription address ....

.... Postcode ....

Gift message (*20 words max. or include your own gift card*):

....

....

Please send *Bible Reflections for Older People* beginning with the September 2022 / January 2023 / May 2023* issue (**delete as appropriate)*:

(*please tick box*)	**UK**	**Europe**	**Rest of world**
Bible Reflections for Older People	☐ £20.25	☐ £27.75	☐ £31.80

Total enclosed £ .... (*cheques should be made payable to 'BRF'*)

Please charge my MasterCard / Visa with £ ....

Card no. ☐☐☐☐ ☐☐☐☐ ☐☐☐☐ ☐☐☐☐

Expires end ☐☐☐☐   Security code ☐☐☐   Last 3 digits on the reverse of the card

We will use your personal data to process this order. From time to time we may send you information about the work of BRF. Please contact us if you wish to discuss your mailing preferences **brf.org.uk/privacy**

Please return this form to:
BRF, 15 The Chambers, Vineyard, Abingdon OX14 3FE | **enquiries@brf.org.uk**
For terms and cancellation information, please visit **brfonline.org.uk/terms**.

Bible Reading Fellowship is a charity (233280) and company limited by guarantee (301324), registered in England and Wales